T0179621

COTTONMOUTH VS. SNAPPING TURTLE

BY NATHAN SOMMER

BELLWETHER MEDIA • MINNEAPOLIS, MN

Torque brims with excitement
perfect for thrill-seekers of all kinds.
Discover daring survival skills, explore
uncharted worlds, and marvel at mighty
engines and extreme sports. In *Torque* books,
anything can happen. Are you ready?

This edition first published in 2025 by Bellwether Media, Inc.

Library of Congress Cataloging-in-Publication Data

LC record for Cottonmouth vs. Snapping Turtle available at:
https://lccn.loc.gov/2024019763

Editor: Suzane Nguyen   Designer: Hunter Demmin

Printed in the United States of America, North Mankato, MN.

TABLE OF CONTENTS

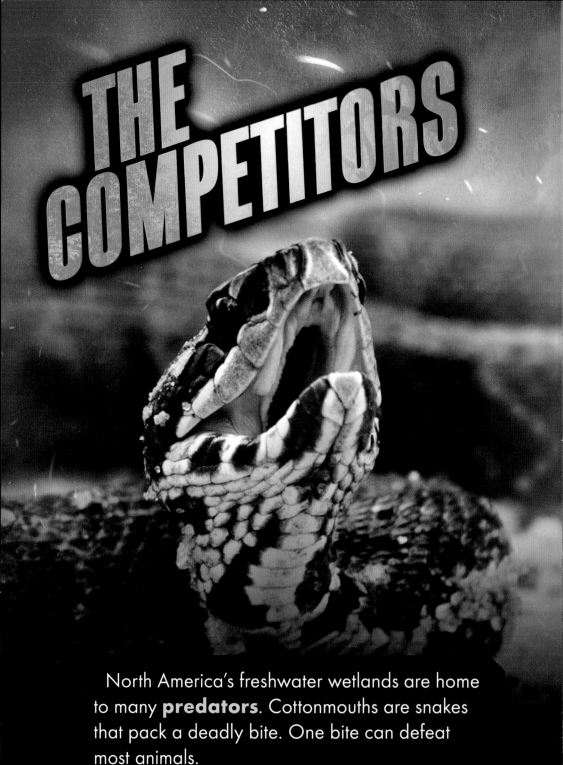

THE COMPETITORS

North America's freshwater wetlands are home to many **predators**. Cottonmouths are snakes that pack a deadly bite. One bite can defeat most animals.

Cottonmouths often share **habitats** with common snapping turtles. These turtles catch **prey** on land and in water. Very few animals escape their powerful jaws. Whose bite is deadlier?

Cottonmouths are the only **venomous** water snakes in North America. They have wide heads. They have thick bodies and brownish-black scales. The largest grow more than 6 feet (1.8 meters) long!

Cottonmouths live throughout the southeastern United States. They can be found in most wetland habitats. The snakes are also called water moccasins.

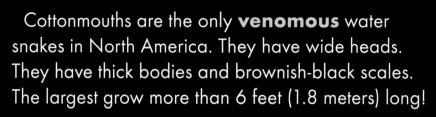

ALL IN A NAME

Cottonmouths are named after the white color inside their mouths. They show this when they are in danger!

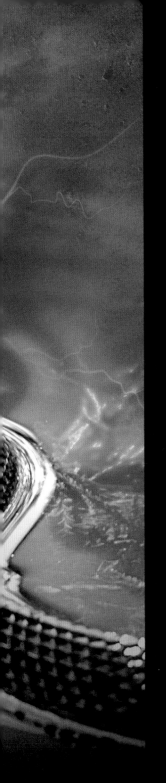

COTTONMOUTH PROFILE

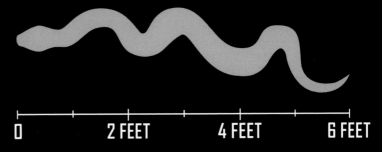

0   2 FEET   4 FEET   6 FEET

LENGTH
MORE THAN 6 FEET
(1.8 METERS)

WEIGHT
UP TO 4 POUNDS
(1.8 KILOGRAMS)

HABITATS

RIVERS   LAKES   SWAMPS

COTTONMOUTH RANGE

█ RANGE

⑦

SNAPPING TURTLE PROFILE

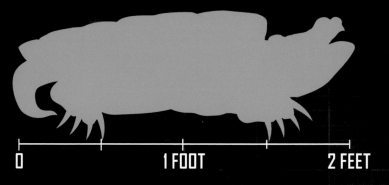

| 0 | 1 FOOT | 2 FEET |

SHELL LENGTH
UP TO 1.5 FEET
(0.5 METERS)

WEIGHT
UP TO 35 POUNDS
(16 KILOGRAMS)

HABITATS

RIVERS

LAKES

SWAMPS

SNAPPING TURTLE RANGE

■ RANGE

Snapping turtles have thick shells and long tails. They can weigh up to 35 pounds (16 kilograms). Their sturdy shells can grow up to 1.5 feet (0.5 meters) long.

Snapping turtles are **solitary** creatures. They live in parts of the United States and Canada. The turtles are mostly found in freshwater wetlands.

SECRET WEAPONS

PIT ORGAN

Cottonmouths have **pit organs** between their eyes and nose. These sense the heat given off by nearby prey. The snakes find prey before prey can even see them!

Snapping turtles have long, sharp claws. They use them to hold and tear apart larger prey. They also use their claws to dig through mud.

CLAWS

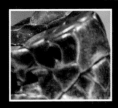  

PIT ORGANS   CAMOUFLAGE   VENOM

Cottonmouths use their brownish-black scales to **camouflage** their long bodies. The snakes are hard to see when slithering through wetlands. This allows them to catch prey by surprise.

SECRET WEAPONS

SHARP CLAWS

LONG,
FLEXIBLE NECKS

POWERFUL,
HOOKED JAWS

Snapping turtles have long, **flexible** necks. They stretch these quickly to **lunge** at prey and enemies. Their necks also help the turtles surface for air when underwater.

Cottonmouths use sharp **fangs** to **inject** prey with deadly venom. The venom stops prey's blood from flowing properly. Cottonmouth bites stop small prey within minutes.

COTTONMOUTH FANG SIZE

0.5 INCHES
(1.3 CENTIMETERS)

BITE FORCE

148 POUNDS PER SQUARE INCH

COMMON SNAPPING TURTLE

162 POUNDS PER SQUARE INCH

HUMAN

Snapping turtles use their powerful, hooked jaws to quickly catch prey. Most prey cannot escape the turtle's deadly **grip**. Their sharp jaws easily tear captured food apart.

ATTACK MOVES

Cottonmouths hunt both on land and in water.
They often wait near shorelines and water holes.
Then, they catch prey by surprise!

Snapping turtles often bury themselves in mud underwater. They cover everything except their eyes and nose. Then, they wait to capture prey that swim too close!

UNDERWATER WINTERS

In winter, snapping turtles can stay underwater for months at a time!

Cottonmouths track meals by scent. Some sniff out and **scavenge** for dead animals. The snakes swallow their meals headfirst!

YOUNG HUNTERS

Baby cottonmouths have bright yellow tails. They use their tails as bait to attract prey.

Snapping turtles can be **aggressive** out of water. They will attack when they are cornered or in danger. Their bites are strong enough to break bones!

A snapping turtle hopes to catch its next meal underwater. Suddenly, a cottonmouth swims above it. The turtle uses its neck to lunge at the snake. It bites the snake.

The snake bites the turtle back! The turtle lets go of the cottonmouth. It is slowly defeated by the snake's venom. The cottonmouth avoids becoming prey today!

GLOSSARY

aggressive—ready to fight

camouflage—to use colors and patterns to help an animal hide in its surroundings

fangs—long, sharp teeth

flexible—able to bend easily without breaking

grip—a tight hold

habitats—the homes or areas where animals prefer to live

inject—to force a fluid into something

lunge—to move forward quickly

pit organs—special body parts that allow snakes to detect the movement of prey in the darkness

predators—animals that hunt other animals for food

prey—animals that are hunted by other animals for food

scavenge—to eat food that is already dead

solitary—related to living alone

venomous—able to produce venom; venom is a kind of poison made by some snakes.

AT THE LIBRARY

Hamilton, Lynn, and Katie Gillespie. *Turtle*. New York, N.Y.: AV2 by Weigl, 2020.

Maurer, Tracey Nelson. *Cottonmouths*. New York, N.Y.: Crabtree Publishing, 2022.

Russo, Kristin. *Reptiles*. Minneapolis, Minn.: Abdo Reference, 2024.

ON THE WEB

FACTSURFER

Factsurfer.com gives you a safe, fun way to find more information.

1. Go to www.factsurfer.com

2. Enter "cottonmouth vs. snapping turtle" into the search box and click 🔍.

3. Select your book cover to see a list of related web sites.

INDEX

The images in this book are reproduced through the courtesy of: Jason Patrick Ross, front cover (cottonmouth); Dan Olsen, front cover (common snapping turtle); Seth LeGrange, pp. 2-3, 14 (main), 20-24; Bruce MacQueen, pp. 2-3, 17, 20-24; Jay Ondreicka, pp. 4, 16; Gerry Bishop, p. 5; jo Crebbin, pp. 6-7; Chase D'animulls, p. 6 (inset); Brain Lasenby, pp. 8-9, 13 (main); Nicole Ramsey, p. 10; Frances Tackaberry, p. 11; Donna Bollenbach, p. 12; Danny Ye, p. 12 (pit organs); Bo Poe, p. 12 (camouflage); James DeBoer, p. 12 (venom); Michele Korfhage, p. 13 (sharp claws); Rejean Aline Bedard, p. 13 (long, flexible necks); Brian Woolman, p. 13; (powerful, hooked jaws); Andrea J Smith, p. 15; Paul S. Wolf, p. 18; Andrew DuBois / Alamy Stock Photo/ Alamy, p. 18 (inset); Dylan Baldwin, p. 19.